THE

WISDOM

OF

SOLOMON

:

ANCIENT TEACHINGS FOR MODERN BUSINESS

Text prepared from the New American
Standard Version of the Bible

Table

of

~ Contents ~

Part I - Character Traits for Success

Part II - Specific Business Practices

Part III - Things to Avoid

Conclusion

~ Part I ~

Character Traits for Success

Introduction

Although Solomon wrote the Book of Proverbs more than 3,000 years ago, the wisdom contained within those teachings is as valuable today as it was in ancient times. Amazingly, the fundamentals for success also have remained the same throughout the centuries. Even in our ever-changing, technological world, Solomon's wisdom applies.

King Solomon was known during his lifetime as the wisest man on earth. Men came . . . **from all the kings of the earth who had heard of his wisdom (1 Kings 4:34). For he was wiser than all men, than Ethan the Ezrahite, Heman, Calcol and Darda, the sons of Mahol; and his fame was known in all the surrounding nations (1 Kings 4:31).** And while the writings of other ancient scholars such as Plato, Socrates, and Aristotle are regularly studied, and the teachings of the Budda, Machiavelli and Sun Tzu speak to today's politicians and businessmen, it remains a mystery why more study has not been devoted to the teachings of the wisest man who ever lived. Solomon's wisdom is attributed to the Heavenly Father and was given to him that it might be transcribed for humanity's use. **In the night that God appeared to Solomon and said to him, Ask what I shall give you, Solomon said to God, Give me now wisdom and knowledge, that I may go out and come in before these people; for who can rule this great people of Thine? And God said to Solomon, Because you had this in mind, and did not ask for riches, wealth, or honor, or the life of those who hate you, nor have you even asked for long life, but you have asked for your-**

self wisdom and knowledge, that you may rule My people, over whom I have made you king, wisdom and knowledge have been granted to you. And I will give you riches and wealth and honor, such as none of the kings who were before you has possessed, nor those who will come after you (II Chronicles 1:7-12).

We have access to this wonderful wisdom; why haven't we searched it out and applied it to our daily lives? 1 Kings 4:32 tells us that Solomon spoke 3000 proverbs and his songs were 1005. He spoke on every facet of life as it existed during his time, around 950 B.C. The expanse of his wisdom is phenomenal and was so well-regarded worldwide that the Queen of Sheba came to witness his wisdom herself and responded,

. . . It was a true report which I heard in my own land about your words and wisdom. Nevertheless I did not believe the reports, until I came and my eyes had seen it. And behold, the half was not told me. You exceed in wisdom and prosperity the report which I heard (I Kings 10:6-7).

The focus of this book is on how Solomon's wisdom relates specifically to business. Solomon spoke directly to the do's and don't's of business practices in ways that are as relevant today as they were in ancient times. However, before moving on to these specifics, let us look at some characteristics Solomon regarded as necessary for success in life in general as well as in business. The following thirteen character traits are given as the keys to a successful life: wisdom, righteousness, hard work, diligence, honesty, humility, insight, integrity, discipline, reflective speech, generosity, reluctance to anger, and prudence.

Wisdom

The underpinning of success in any endeavor is wisdom. The entire foundation of Solomon's life was built around the search for wisdom. **And I set my mind to seek and explore by wis- dom concerning all that has been done under heaven. It is a grievous task which God has given to the sons of men to be afflicted with** (Ecclesiastes 1:13). However, he found wisdom does not lead to happiness; indeed, quite the contrary is true. **And I set my mind to know wisdom and to know madness and folly; I realized that this also is striving after wind. Because in much wisdom there is much grief, and increasing knowledge results in increasing pain** (Ecclesiastes 1:17-18).

Even with increasing grief and pain, Solomon still cites wisdom as the key to success. **How blessed is the man who finds wisdom, And the man who gains understanding. For its profit is better than the profit of silver, and its gain than fine gold** (Proverbs 3:13-14).

Solomon is also very specific about where wisdom originates. **He says, The fear of the Lord is the beginning of knowledge; Fools despise wisdom and instruction** (Proverbs 1:7).

He speaks about how to obtain wisdom. **My son, observe the commandment of your father, And do not forsake the teaching of your mother. Bind them continually on your heart; Tie them around your neck** (Proverbs 6:20-21). This is to say that traditions are important in the process of acquiring wisdom. **A wise** man will hear and increase in learning, and a man of under- standing will acquire counsel (Proverbs 1:5). All men should seek advice and not rely solely on their own knowledge. Solomon goes on to say, **Give instruction to a wise man, and he will be still wiser, Teach a righteous man, and he will increase his learning** (Proverbs 9:9). He again reiterates the value of wisdom: **How much better it is to get wisdom than gold! And to get understanding is to be chosen above silver** (Proverbs 16:16).

Finally, Solomon adds the rewards of wisdom: For wisdom is protection just as money is protection. But the advantage of knowledge is that wisdom preserves the lives of its possessors (Ecclesiastes 7:12). And, **The crown of the wise is their riches, But the folly of fools is foolishness** (Proverbs 14:24).

Righteousness

Righteousness is probably the hardest of all the characteristics to pinpoint because it encompasses several different traits.

Righteousness, as described in the Proverbs of Solomon, is a very basic element that relates to honesty, integrity, fairness, sincerity, and kindness. As we would say about a righteous individual, "He/She is a good person." Solomon contrasts the righteous to the wicked: The righteous is concerned for the rights of the poor. The wicked does not understand such concern (Proverbs 29:7). Although he recognized that, **Indeed, there is not a righteous man on earth who continually does good and who never sins (Ecclesiastes 7:20).**

Solomon used the following proverbs to acknowledge specific business rewards that go to the righteous: Adversity pursues sinners, **But the righteous will be rewarded with prosperity. A good man leaves an inheritance to his children's children, And the wealth of the sinner is stored up for the righteous (Proverbs 13:21-22). The wicked earns deceptive wages, But he who sows righteousness gets a true reward (Proverbs 11:18). Ill- gotten gains do not profit, But righteousness delivers from death (Proverbs 10:2). The wages of the righteous is life, The income of the wicked, punishment (Proverbs 10:16). The right- eous has enough to satisfy his appetite, But the stomach of the wicked is want (Proverbs 13:25).**

And while the rewards of righteousness are spelled out well, so are the punishments for the wicked because, **When the righteous triumph, there is great glory, But when the wicked rise, men hide themselves** (Proverbs 28:12). The righteousness of the blameless will smooth his way, But the wicked will fall by his own wickedness. The righteousness of the upright will deliver them, But the treacherous will be caught by their own greed (Proverbs 11:5-6.) The wicked desires the booty of evil men, But the root of the righteous yields fruit (Proverbs 12:12). **And finally, He who trusts in his riches will fall, But the righteous will flourish like the green leaf** (Proverbs 11:28).

Solomon sums up the importance of righteousness in business: **Better is a little with righteousness than great income with injustice (Proverbs 16:8).**

Hard Work

In no uncertain terms, Solomon lays out the importance hard work plays in achieving success in business, as well as the con- sequences for failure to work hard. He says, **He who tills his land will have plenty of food, But he who follows empty pursuits will have poverty in plenty** (Proverbs 28:19).

Hard work follows only wisdom and righteousness in terms of importance to success. Solomon uses the analogy of the ant as an example: **Go to the ant, O sluggard, Observe her ways and be wise, Which having no chief, Officer or ruler, prepares her food in the summer, And gathers her provisions in the harvest. How long will you lie down, O Sluggard? When will you arise from your sleep? A little sleep, a little slumber, A little fold- ing of the hands to rest—And your poverty will come in like a vagabond, And your need like an armed man (Proverbs 6:6- 11).**

Solomon realized that the brightest of plans and best of intentions will not earn one dime without implementation. As he explains, **In all labor there is profit, But mere talk leads only to poverty (Proverbs 14: 23).**

Some very capable people are never successful because they talk a good game but never actually put any of their capabilities to work. Of these people, Solomon says, **He who tills his land will have plenty of bread, But he who pursues vain things lacks sense (Proverbs 12:11).**

This takes the concept of hard work a step further. One should not only work hard on things to accomplish, but one should also avoid working on things that will not produce a positive result.

Solomon not only warns against slack in ourselves, but tells of the danger that laziness in others presents. He states, **The way of the sluggard is a hedge of thorns, But the path of the upright is a highway (Proverbs 15:19).** He goes on to say, **The sluggard does not plow after the autumn, So he begs during the harvest and has nothing (Proverbs 20:4).**

Furthermore, in two direct references to lazy employees, Solomon cautions: **He also who is slack in his work Is brother to him who destroys (Proverbs 18:9).** Also, **Like vinegar to the teeth and smoke to the eyes, So is the lazy one to those who send him (Proverbs 10:26).**

Solomon gives three last warnings: **Laziness casts into a deep sleep, And an idle man will suffer hunger (Proverbs 19:15); The desire of the sluggard puts him to death, For his hands refuse to work (Proverbs 21:25);** and **Do not love sleep, lest you become poor; Open your eyes, and you will be satisfied with food (Proverbs 20:13).**

There is no doubt that, from ancient Israel to modern America, throughout all time, hard work pays off.

Diligence

Diligence is the fourth character trait Solomon points out. Wisdom, righteousness, and hard work must be applied consistently. Success is dependent on a straightforward and dedicated commitment to achieving the task at hand. **Let your eyes look directly ahead, And let your gaze be fixed straight in front of you. Watch the path of your feet, And all your ways will be established. Do not turn to the right nor to the left; Turn your foot from evil** (Proverbs 4:25-27).

Success in business is a long-range proposition, not a one-shot deal. How many business people have we seen who are "flashes in the pan," here today and gone tomorrow? As Solomon explains, **A faithful man will abound with blessings, But he who makes haste to be rich will not go unpunished** (Proverbs 28:20).

Solomon was obviously aware that get-rich-quick schemes did not work in 1000 B.C. nor will they today. **The plans of the diligent lead surely to advantage, But everyone who is hasty comes surely to poverty** (Proverbs 21:5).

Solomon contrasts diligence with laziness and explains the gains and losses between the two. **The soul of the sluggard craves and gets nothing, But the soul of the diligent is made fat** (Proverbs 13:4). Further, **The land of the diligent will rule, But the slack hand will be put to forced labor** (Proverbs 12:24).

The one thing all truly successful business people have in com- mon is an almost fanatical commitment to accomplishing their goals. It is as if they have blinders on, like horses at the race track. Their eyes on the goal straight ahead of them, they pursue it consistently, day in and day out, with no deviation.

Solomon had a keen understanding of the relationship between diligence and business and was aware of the rewards that come with diligence.

He is blunt in his statement, **Poor is he who works with a negligent hand, But the hand of the diligent makes rich (Proverbs 10:4)**.

Honesty

There are some specific proverbs regarding the role of honesty in business, but Solomon also has made some general statements about honesty as a character trait and the rewards it brings. He says, **Better is the poor who walks in his integrity, Than he who is crooked though he be rich (Proverbs 28:6)**. He also says, **He who walks blamelessly will be delivered But he who is crooked will fall all at once (Proverbs 28:18)**.

The concept of honesty is pointed out time and again by Solomon: **A false balance is an abomination to the Lord, But a just weight is His delight (Proverbs 11:1)**. Differing weights and differing measures, Both of them are abominable to the Lord (Proverbs 20:10). Differing weights are an abomination to the Lord, And a false scale is not good (Proverbs 20:23). The same proverb is repeated three times, not only for effect, but to emphasize the widespread problem that existed in Solomon's time with a lack of ethics in business.

Another aspect of honesty is truth. **What is desirable in a man is his kindness, And it is better to be a poor man than a liar (Proverbs 19:22). Bread obtained by falsehood is sweet to a man, But afterward, his mouth will be filled with gravel (Proverbs 20:17). The getting of treasures by a lying tongue Is a fleeting vapor, the pursuit of death (Proverbs 21:6). True full lips will be established forever, But a lying tongue is only for a moment (Proverbs 12:19)**.

Although it may appear that dishonest tactics might be useful in the short run, they are bound to bring problems and even destruction in the long run. Over time, lies will be found out, but honesty will be rewarded. Solomon speaks to the short-term gains of falsehoods when he writes, **He who profits illicitly troubles his own house, But he who hate bribes will live (Proverbs 15:27).** Solomon also tells of the reward for dishonesty: **And your poverty will come in like a vagabond, and your need like an armed man (Proverbs 6:11).**

Humility

Solomon refers many times to the importance of humility as a key to success. In today's society, too often we confuse wealth with success. Apparently, the same thing occurred in ancient Jerusalem, for Solomon wrote, **The rich man is wise in his own eyes, But the poor who has understanding sees through him (Proverbs 28:11).**

Solomon knew that wealth was only the beginning of success; to be truly successful, one must obtain honor, and the key to honor is humility. As he noted, **The fear of the Lord is the instruction for wisdom, And before honor comes humility (Proverbs 15:33). Therefore, Do not be wise in your own eyes; Fear the Lord and turn away from evil (Proverbs 3:7). He continues: If you are wise, you are wise for yourself, And if you scoff, you alone will bear it (Proverbs 9:12). It is not good to eat much honey, Nor is it glory to search out one's own glory (Proverbs 25:27). So, Let another praise you, and not your own mouth; A stranger, and not your own lips (Proverbs 27:2).**

Finally, Solomon tells of the dangers that come with pride and the rewards that come with humility. **A man's pride will bring him low, But a humble spirit will obtain honor (Proverbs 29:23). The reward of humility and the fear of the Lord are riches, honor and life (Proverbs 22:4).**

Insight

Solomon said, **A man will be praised according to his insight, But** one of **perverse mind will** be **despised (Proverbs 12:8)**. Insight, a gift or a blessing of character, is the ability to view a subject and see beneath the surface. Insight is developed through experience; it comes from learning from the lessons life offers. It might be defined as a true depth of understand- ing. The opposite would be the refusal to seek understanding, to perversely insist on keeping a narrow, selfish field of vision. And, as Solomon said, "a man will be praised for his insight."

Integrity

In all of Solomon's proverbs, only one verse directly addresses integrity: **He who walks in integrity walks securely, But he who perverts his ways will be found out (Proverbs 10:9).** Although the word itself is mentioned only once, it is the theme and the focus of all Solomon's teachings.

Webster defines integrity as "the state of being entire; whole- ness; probity; honesty." Since all of Solomon's proverbs deal indirectly with integrity, it is possible that he sought to avoid any misinterpretation of a vague concept and chose more specific words for his teachings. However, the lesson to be learned from this verse is that we are to strive to be whole in terms of all the other character traits Solomon has addressed sowe may truly "walk in integrity."

Discipline

Poverty and shame will come to him who neglects discipline, But he who regards reproof will be honored (Proverbs 13:18).

From the time of childhood, discipline is one of the hardest things for an individual to accept. But as we grow older, we come to realize that parental discipline was for our own good. Solomon, in numerous verses throughout Proverbs and Ecclesiastes, addresses the subject, with discipline of children being the most notable. **He who spares his rod hates his son, But he who loves him disciplines him diligently (Proverbs 13:24).**

However, the verse, Poverty and shame will come to him who neglects discipline, but he who regards reproof will be honored, speaks to an adult discipline. A discipline that, when heeded, adds to honor, and when neglected leads to poverty and shame.

In business, discipline is the glue that holds all the other character traits together. Without discipline to set a goal and see it through, all is lost. It is the familiar tale of the salesman who always sells but never makes any money because he lacks the discipline to see that the orders get filled and the invoices get delivered and paid. Time and again we see the best potential salesmen in the world fail because of their lack of discipline in making calls every day and following through with the paperwork.

Discipline is very similar to diligence. Discipline goes a step further, however, in that it becomes a way of life. More than the "stick to it" attitude characterized by diligence, discipline is a total resolve to follow through on every minute detail, not just the larger task at hand.

Discipline comes from within, and it can also come from out- side forces. However, it is even more difficult to accept discipline from others, and Solomon realized this fact of nature. Proverbs 13:18 points out that, . . . **He who regards reproof will be honored.** As a practical matter, the ability to accept discipline in the workplace from one's superiors is a vital key to success. Accept discipline graciously and move forward with knowledge gained.

Reflective Speech

Solomon addresses the importance of speech (more familiar to us, perhaps, is the term *communication*). It, more often than any other characteristic, is vital to success in business. One adjective could serve as synopsis of all the verses, and that is reflective. Being reflective means that we should always think (reflect) before we speak: **He who restrains his words has knowledge, And he who has a cool spirit has understanding (Proverbs 17:27).**

Wisdom, humility, and insight are all reflected through our speech. **On the lips of the discerning, wisdom is found, But a rod is for the back of him who lacks understanding. Wise men store up knowledge, But with the mouth of the foolish, ruin is at hand (Proverbs 10:13-14).**

Speech includes not only what we say, but also what we don't say. **Even a fool, when he keeps silent, is considered wise; When he closes his lips, he is counted prudent (Proverbs 17:28).** I can remember my father telling me as a child, "Keep your mouth shut and people won't know how dumb you are." (Little did I realize at the time that he was actually quoting an ancient proverb that has been true from the beginning of time.)

In Proverbs 21:23, Solomon gives us the summation of the value of reflective speech, **He who guards his mouth and his tongue, guards his soul from trouble.** Solomon considered the mouth and tongue the passageway to the very soul of man and the means to wisdom: **The lips of the wise spread knowledge, But the hearts of fools are not so (Proverbs 15:7)**. And the wisdom of reflective speech will not go unrewarded: **A man will be satisfied with good by the fruit of his words, And the deeds of a man's hand will return to him (Proverbs 12:14)**.

In addition to the wisdom and rewards of reflective speech, Solomon also tells of the problems and punishments of the two most notable evils of speech: gossiping and lying. He says of lying, **A false witness will not go unpunished, And he who tells lies will perish (Proverbs 19:9)**. He also states, **He who conceals hatred has lying lips, And he who spreads slander is a fool. When there are many words, transgression is unavoidable, But he who restrains his lips is wise (Proverbs 10:18-19)**. He also warns of gossiping: **He who despises his neighbour lacks sense, But a man of understanding keeps silent. He who goes about as a talebearer reveals secrets, But he who is trustworthy conceals a matter (Proverbs 11:12-13)**.

Solomon was very specific that unreflective speech was a sure way to man's downfall: **He who has a crooked mind finds no good, And he who is perverted in his language falls into evil (Proverbs 17:20)**. He also states, **A lying tongue hates those it crushes, And a flattering mouth works ruin (Proverbs 26:28)**.

While gossiping and lying are certainly terrible actions, and none of us would openly go around lying about people to do deliberate harm, Solomon in all his infinite wisdom, in one simple verse, shows how easily we all fall into this trap: **The words of a whisperer are like dainty morsels, And they go** down into the innermost part of the body (Proverbs 26:22). Let us not be whisperers, but let us use reflective speech as we search for success.

Generosity

In today's business world, the most often quoted motto is "You've got to look out for Old Number One." Taking care of one's own needs and desires comes first, and after that maybe we can worry about others. The problem with this approach is that we never quite get past worrying about ourselves so that we have time to care about others.

Based on the many proverbs that Solomon addresses to generosity, one gets the feeling that maybe times have not changed so much, and that maybe looking out for Old Number One was as much a problem in Solomon's time as it is today. Solomon points out, not just the need to be generous, but also the rewards that are directly related to helping those less fortunate than ourselves.

Honor the Lord from your wealth, And from the first of all your produce; So your barns will be filled with plenty, And your vats will overflow with new wine (Proverbs 3:9-10). Notice that Solomon doesn't say honor the church with your wealth: he says honor the Lord! I raise this point to emphasize that all we have should be used in ways that honor the Lord. Yes, we should donate to the church from the first of our produce, but blessings come when we honor the Lord from our wealth.

Solomon continues throughout Proverbs to tell of the rewards of generosity in earthly giving, and if we extract the verses on generosity from Chapter 3 through Chapter 28, it reads as a classroom lecture from the King himself. Do not withhold good from those to whom it is due, **When it is in your power to do it. Do not say to your neighbor, 'Go, and come back, And** tomorrow I will give it,' When you have it with you. Do not devise harm against your neighbor, while he lives in security beside you (Proverbs 3:27-29). The generous man will be prosperous, And he who waters will himself be watered. He who withholds grain, the people will curse him, But blessings will be on the head of him who sells it (Proverbs 11:25-26). He who despises his neighbor sins, But happy is he who is gracious to the poor (Proverbs 14:21). He who mocks the poor reproaches his Maker; He who rejoices at calamity will not go unpunished (Proverbs 17:5). He who is gracious to a poor man lends to the Lord, And He will repay him for his good deed (Proverbs 19:17). He who shuts his ear to the cry of the poor Will also cry himself and not be answered (Proverbs 21:13). He who is generous will be blessed, for he gives some of his food to the poor (Proverbs 22:9). He who oppresses the poor to make much for himself Or who gives to the rich, Will only come to poverty (Proverbs 22:16).

Always the professor, Solomon would be remiss in not remind- ing us of the punishment for not heeding his lecture. He warns, **He who gives to the poor will never want, But he who shuts his** eyes will have many curses (Proverbs 28:27).

Reluctance to Anger

According to Solomon, the twelfth characteristic needed for success is that of being slow to anger; he also warns us not to associate with those who do not have this characteristic. **Do not associate with a man given to anger, Or go with a hot-tempered man, Lest you learn his ways, And find a snare for yourself (Proverbs 22:24-25).**

Unfortunately, it seems successful, goal-oriented personalities are often quick-tempered. Solomon says, **He who is slow to anger has great understanding, But he who is quick-tempered exalts folly (Proverbs 14:29).** He also states, **A hot-tempered man stirs up strife, But the slow to anger pacifies contention (Proverbs 15:18).**

An important businessman, very success-oriented, won the campaign for mayor of his hometown. The first few council meetings proceeded without incident. However, when the first major controversy arose, the successful businessman-mayor exhibited a side of his personality that none of his constituents had seen before: he "blew his cool." He ranted and raved and screamed and shouted; it was an amazing scene that left those in the council chamber (news media included) dumfounded.

His temper, which had been latent for years, was brought out by the conflicts involved in political life. His temper was such a problem that he sought psychological help. His psychiatrist had some sage wisdom that would have impressed Solomon himself. His prescription was as follows: Any time you feel yourself being drawn into a controversy that may cause your temper to explode, just ask to be excused and walk around the block, calm down, and then return to deal with the problem in a rational manner. This was an effective way to avoid another embarrassing outburst of emotion.

Solomon saw the same personality problems during his reign. He writes, **Do not be eager in your heart to be angry, For anger resides in the bosom of fools (Ecclesiastes 7:9)**. The following verse leads one to believe that a quick temper may even have been a personality trait of Solomon himself: **A fool always loses his temper, But a wise man holds it back (Proverbs 29:11)**. Solomon doesn't say a wise man never loses his temper; he says he holds it back.

So the next time, before you shout at a business associate or a family member, take a walk around the block. I'm sure Solomon did so as well, probably on numerous occasions.

Prudence

The final character trait required for success is prudence.

A prudent person is cautious and judicious, selective, careful, not extravagant. This is how we should approach life, for Solomon says, **The naive believes everything, But the prudent man considers his steps. The naive inherit folly, But the prudent are crowned with knowledge (Proverbs 14:15,18).**

While Solomon tells us not to be naive about the real world and taken in by it, he also tells us what to do when we con- front it in two very similar verses: **The prudent sees the evil and hides himself, But the naive go on, and are punished for it (Proverbs 22:3)**, and **A prudent man sees evil and hides him- self, The naive proceed and pay the penalty (Proverbs 27:12).**

~ Part II ~

Specific Business Practices

Introduction

Solomon was fairly general in describing the characteristics that one must possess to be successful in all aspects of life. He was much more specific in his outline for a successful business career. Solomon believed that of all things in life, the single most satisfying is one's work. He wrote, **There is nothing better for a man than to eat and drink and tell himself that his labor is good. This also I have seen, that it is from the hand of God (Ecclesiastes 2:24)**. But Solomon warns of the dangers of chasing wealth instead of enjoying one's work: **There was a certain man without a dependent, having neither a son nor a brother, yet there was no end to all his labor. Indeed, his eyes were not satisfied with riches and he never asked, ' . . . And for whom am I laboring and depriving myself of pleasure?' This too is vanity and it is a grievous task (Ecclesiastes 4:8).**

Contrary to popular belief, Solomon never said money is the root of all evil. He did, however, warn of the dangers the love of money brings. He who loves money will not be satisfied with money, nor he who loves abundance with increase. This too is vanity. When goods increase, those who consume them increase. So what is the advantage to their owners except to look on? The sleep of the working man is pleasant, whether he eats little or much. But the full stomach of the rich man does not allow him to sleep.

There is a grievous evil which I have seen under the sun: riches being hoarded by their owner to his hurt. When those riches were lost through a bad investment and he had fathered

a son, there was nothing to support him. As he had come naked from his mother's womb, so will he return as he came. He will take nothing from the fruit of his labor that he can carry in his hand. And this also is a grievous evil—exactly as a man is born, thus will he die. So, what is the advantage to him who toils for the wind? Throughout his life he also eats in darkness with great vexation, sickness and anger (Ecclesiastes 5:10-17).

What a dark and gloomy picture Solomon paints of those who work only for money and its accumulation. He goes on to explain the true rewards of work and gives us the answer to attaining abundant life: Here is what I have seen to be good and fitting: to eat, to drink and to enjoy oneself in all one's labor in which he toils under the sun during the few days of his life which God has given; for this is his reward. Furthermore, as for every man to whom God has given riches and wealth, **He has also empowered him to eat from them and to receive his reward and rejoice in his labor; this is the gift of God. For he will not often consider the years of his life, because God keeps him occupied with the gladness of his heart** (Ecclesiastes 5:18-20).

So, as we delve into the specific business practices Solomon set forth, let us keep in perspective that the end result we seek is not wealth and fame, but abundant life.

Protect Your Good Name

The first key Solomon mentioned to attaining a successful career is having a good name. **A good name is to be more desired than great riches, Favor is better than silver and gold (Proverbs 22:1)**. A good name is built over years of commitment to honesty, integrity, and the other character traits we have mentioned earlier. **A good name is better than a good ointment, And the day of one's death is better than the day of one's birth (Ecclesiastes 7:1)**.

In today's business world, there is a term used in putting a dollar value on a good name: goodwill. It is commonplace in selling a business to ask a purchase price for the goodwill built by the business. Hopefully, from a personal perspective the value of our goodwill exceeds the value of our inventory.

Seek a Good Mate

We have heard it said that "behind every great man there is a great woman." Although the saying may be hackneyed, there is no doubt that Solomon considered a good mate to be extremely important in a successful life. **An excellent wife is the crown of her husband, But she who shames him is as rottenness in his bones (Proverbs 12:4).**

As we enter into the twenty-first century, women are just as involved in their business careers as men. The word *spouse* can be substituted for *woman* and *wife* in the verses that deal with marriage and the relevant point is retained. **It is better to live in a corner of a roof, Than in a house shared with a contentious woman (Proverbs 21:9). It is better to live in a desert land, than with a contentious and vexing woman (Proverbs 21:19).**

What Solomon saw in the marital relationship and its relation to business was, **Two are better than one because they have a good return for their labor. For if either of them falls, the one will lift up his companion. But woe to the one who falls when there is not another to lift him up (Ecclesiastes 4:9-10).** Solomon truly realized the need of support at home to help make it through those tough times in the workplace. **Houses and wealth are an inheritance from fathers, But a prudent wife is from the Lord (Proverbs 19:14).**

Seek Good Partners

Just as Solomon saw a need for a good partner in the home, he also recognized that quality partners in the workplace are vital. **Iron sharpens iron, So one man sharpens another** (Proverbs 27:17). Also, **He who walks with wise men will be wise, But the companion of fools will suffer harm** (Proverbs 13:20).

In the business world of today, the need for partners still remains strong. Strangely, the best partners are sometimes very opposite in personalities and character traits; the value of the partnership lies in their ability to build on each others' strengths and weaknesses.

A man of many friends comes to ruin, But there is a friend who sticks closer than a brother (Proverbs 18:24). Solomon warns against having too many partners. Apparently there are only a certain number of close personal relationships an individual can handle at a time; and while this number may vary for each individual, there is a maximum number for everyone. An example of the value of limiting close business relationships may be seen in the law firm that started out with two partners; over the years they grew and prospered, taking in new partners each year. Eventually, the two original partners realized there were partners of the firm they didn't even know, and the firm had taken on an entirely different personality that they didn't necessarily like or were able to control.

In giving guidelines to partners, Solomon is actually much more specific about whom not to choose as partners. **He who is a partner with a thief hates his own life; He hears the oath but tells nothing (Proverbs 29:24). He who goes about as a slanderer reveals secrets, Therefore do not associate with a gossip (Proverbs 20:19).**

Further, A worthless person, a wicked man, **Is the one who walks with a false mouth, Who winks with his eyes, who signals with his feet, who points with his fingers; Who with perversity in his heart devises evil continually, who spreads strife. Therefore his calamity will come suddenly; Instantly he will be broken, and there will be no healing (Proverbs 6:12-15).**

Finding good partners today would not be so hard if we would only take the time to make sure they do not possess any of the above traits. For, **Like a bad tooth and an unsteady foot Is confidence in a faithless man in time of trouble (Proverbs 25:19).**

A favorite story concerns falling in with the wrong partners. Solomon warns, **My son, if sinners entice you, do not consent. If they say, 'Come with us, Let us lie in wait for blood, let us ambush the innocent without cause; Let us swallow them alive like Sheol, Even whole, as those who go down to the pit; We shall find all kinds of precious wealth, We shall fill our houses with spoil; Throw in your lot with us, We shall all have one purse,' My son, do not walk in the way with them. Keep your feet from their path, For their feet run to evil, And they hasten to shed blood. Indeed, it is useless to spread the net In the eyes of any bird; But they lie in wait for their own blood; They ambush their own lives. So are the ways of every-**

one who gains by violence; It takes away the life of its possessors (Proverbs 1:10-19).

There is no doubt that Solomon had seen the destruction wrought by bad partners and the value of good partners. Let us heed his advice and be diligent in our selection of business partners.

Seek Counsel

Along with a good name, a good spouse, and good partners, Solomon encourages us to seek counsel. **Incline your ear and hear the words of the wise, And apply your mind to my knowledge; For it will be pleasant if you keep them within you, That they** may be ready on your lips (Proverbs 22:17-18).

Solomon also tells us where to seek counsel. **The glory of young men is their strength, And the honor of old men is their gray hair** (Proverbs 20:29). **A gray head is a crown of glory; It is found in the way of righteousness** (Proverbs 16:31). Solomon knew then, as we should today, that experience is the best teacher. So, as we seek consultation, it should be from those who have been there before.

During media coverage of a conflict in the Middle East, one of the military arms "experts" sounded very impressive until he made the comment, "Well, I've never actually been in combat before." I immediately changed the channel; if I am going to seek knowledge, I want it from someone who's been there.

Solomon expounded on the need for counsel. **The way of a fool is right in his own eyes, But a wise man is he who listens to counsel** (Proverbs 12:15). **Through presumption nothing comes but strife, But with those who receive counsel is wisdom** (Proverbs 13:10).

Each of us needs a sounding board in our business life, some- one to bounce our ideas off and see how rational or ridiculous they might be. That sounding board, whether it be our good spouse, good partner, or just good friend, has to have two characteristics: they must be trustworthy and not share our ideas with anyone else, and they must be completely honest with us and tell us if our ideas are ridiculous.

Once I worked for a man who eventually moved on to another company. During the time he was my boss, I did not appreciate his true role; for he was very lenient, and I would sometimes go for weeks without checking in with him. After he was gone though, I realized what a truly valuable resource I had lost. He had been my sounding board and my counsel, and without his steady presence I struggled for quite some time.

Solomon tells us, **Without consultation, plans are frustrated, But with many counselors they succeed (Proverbs 15:22).**

Make Plans

Where there is no vision, the people are unrestrained, but happy is he who keeps the law (Proverbs 29:18). Goals and visions are imperative for success in business. Without goals, one floats aimlessly about like a ship without a rudder. To set and attain goals, one must devise a plan of action. In essence, our plans serve as our rudder to keep us on course.

It is very easy in life to just "go with the flow," take the path of least resistance. However, if you do not set goals and establish a plan of action your full potential will never be realized, and that would be a loss and a shame.

Solomon realized the difficulty in setting plans and sticking to them. He said, **A plan in the heart of a man is like deep water, But a man of understanding draws it out. (Proverbs 20:5)**. There is nothing in life any harder than sticking to a plan. That is why we need not only long-term business plans but also short-term plans that can be monitored on a weekly or even daily basis. Short-term plans are pathways to our long- term goals.

Once we have established our plans, we should proceed forward on a diligent course. Solomon cautions, **Do not say, 'Why is it that the former days were better than these?' For it is not from wisdom that you ask about this (Ecclesiastes 7:10)**.

As we pursue our plans, we will be met with turmoil; sometimes it will seem that the more we accomplish, the tougher the challenges become. But as the course becomes rugged, we must remember Solomon's two assurances: **Commit your works to the Lord, And your plans will be established (Proverbs 16:3).** And, **The mind of man plans his way, But the Lord directs his steps (Proverbs 16:9).**

Solomon also advised, **Prepare plans by consultation, and make war by wise guidance (Proverbs 20:18).** Business is our equivalent to Solomon's war. Every day we face trials and tribulation not dissimilar to those of the battlefield. If we have our plan structured with wise consultation and stick to that plan, our chances of victory increase tremendously.

Hone Your Skills

As we prepare our plan for business, we should be ever mindful of our own personal skills. Solomon, in his ancient wisdom, sees forever clearly: **Do you see a man skilled in his work? He will stand before kings; He will not stand before obscure men (Proverbs 22:29).** Our first priority in planning should be to identify those things in which we excel, so that we may master whatever profession we choose. Know your job or profession inside and out. To be a success in business, know your business. Any job worth doing is worth doing well. Only your best is good enough.

Obtain Capital

The obsessive need for capital would seem to be a recent phenomenon of our economic society, but Solomon foresaw: **That which has been is that which will be, And that which has been done is that which will be done. So, there is nothing new under the sun. Is there anything of which one might say 'see this, it is new?' Already it has existed for ages Which were before us (Ecclesiastes 1:9-10).** Over 3000 years ago Solomon uttered the remarkable statement, Men prepare a meal for enjoyment, and wine makes life merry, and money is the answer to everything (Ecclesiastes 10:19).

Capital was as important to success then as it is now. So when the Wall Street bankers say, "If we only had more capital we could succeed," don't be tricked into thinking this is a new problem. The need for capital in business has always been and always will be an obstacle to overcome. Solomon was even more direct: **The rich man's wealth is his fortress, the ruin of the poor is their poverty (Proverbs 10:15).** He even saw that as one attains wealth one attains new sets of friends. **Wealth adds many friends, But a poor man is separated from his friend.**

{Proverbs 19:4}.

Solomon also saw the inherent dangers of instant wealth. **A rich man's wealth is his strong city, And like a high wall in his own imagination (Proverbs 18:11).** He added, **An inheritance gained hurriedly at the beginning, Will not be blessed in the end (Proverbs 20:21).**

As always, the way to attain capital that lasts in our day and time is by hard work and saving over time.

Solomon had one other proverb pertaining to capital that we should take as food for thought: **There is one who pretends to be rich, but has nothing; Another pretends to be poor, but has great wealth (Proverbs 13:7).**

Avoid Debt

As Solomon realized the need for capital, he also vividly warned of the dangers of debt and particularly of signing as surety for debt for others. A man lacking in sense pledges, **And becomes surety in the presence of his neighbor (Proverbs 17:18). Take his garment when he becomes surety for a stranger; And for foreigners hold him in pledge (Proverbs 20:16). Do not be among those who give pledges, Among those who become sureties for debts. If you have nothing with which to pay, Why should he take your bed from under you? (Proverbs 22:26-27).**

In today's business world we should never think of consigning notes in partnership agreements. If you have, Solomon tells what action to take: **My son, if you have become surety for your neighbor, have given a pledge for a stranger, If you have been snared with the words of your mouth, Have been caught with the words of your mouth, Do this then, my son, and deliver yourself; Since you have come into the hand of your neighbor, Go, humble yourself, and importune your neighbor. Do not give sleep to your eyes, nor slumber to your eyelids; Deliver your- self like a gazelle from the hunter's hand, And like a bird from the hand of the fowler (Proverbs 6:1-5).**

Obviously, borrowing money is sometimes a necessity. But we should always be mindful not to overextend ourselves to the point of being unable to pay it back. Also, should we go into a business venture with partners, it would be wise for the partners to borrow their shares individually and not cosign each others' notes. Because, as Solomon said, **He who is surety for a stranger will surely suffer for it, But he who hates going surety is safe. (Proverbs 11:15).**

Diversify

One of the recent buzzwords of business is *diversification*. Economists have realized that the old cliché about the dangers of having "all your eggs in one basket" is true; to be successful one must broaden one's base of operation to include multiple product lines or venture into other businesses totally different in scope than the core business of the company. Strangely enough, Solomon taught the value of diversification three thou- sand years ago: **Cast your bread upon the surface of the waters, for you will find it after many days. Divide your portion to seven or even eight, for you do not know what misfortune may occur on the earth (Ecclesiastes 11:1-2).**

Not only was Solomon in favor of diversification, he went so far as to give an actual number as the ideal for divisions. The reason for those numbers is that Solomon knew that a human being can digest only a certain amount of knowledge. Prior to diversifying, we must have a working knowledge of the other lines of business we are considering, and Solomon saw the maximum number of knowledge fields for a person as seven or eight.

Take Inventory

Solomon knew full well the value and need of keeping inventory. The ability we enjoy of keeping unbelievably accurate inventory on computers could lead to complacency. We run a risk by accepting those numbers at face value without delving deeper into their meaning and considering the effect current inventory has on the long-range health of our business. Solomon has sage advice on the reasons for taking inventory: **Know well the condition of your flocks, And pay attention to your herds; For riches are not forever, Nor does a crown endure to all generations. When the grass disappears, the new growth is seen, And the herbs of the mountains are gathered in (Proverbs 27:23-25).**

Abide by the Law

Solomon expresses that we should live within the boundaries of the law in our business dealings and he means it literally. **Do not move the ancient boundary which your fathers have set (Proverbs 22:28).** Also: **Do not move the ancient boundary, or go into the fields of the fatherless (Proverbs 23:10).**

Solomon went one step further to emphasize the importance of operating within the law. **Those who forsake the law praise the wicked, But those who keep the law strive with them. Evil men do not understand justice, But those who seek the Lord under- stand all things (Proverbs 28:4-5).** When your competitors begin skirting around the law to gain an advantage, remember Solomon's promise that the law-abiding will be able to contend with them and those who break the law will be confronted with justice.

Invest in Research and
Development

An intriguing verse that encourages us to budget funds for R & D areas of our business comes in Ecclesiastes 11, verse 6: **Sow your seed in the morning, and do not be idle in the evening, for you do not know whether morning or evening sowing will succeed, or whether both of them alike will be good.** To be successful in business, Solomon realized the need for experimentation to determine which method of planting would produce the most yield. We see the continued need for research and development today and should continue to pursue the method that will produce the most yield.

Recognize the Importance
of Luck and Timing

The two final ingredients Solomon factors into his recipe for a successful life are the two over which man himself has no con- trol: luck and timing. **The lot puts an end to contentions, And decides between the mighty (Proverbs 18:18).** A very successful business man, worth millions, once divulged the following advice to a young protégé: "Young man, you can work as hard and long as you want, and it may make you a good living; but there is only one way anyone ever makes the kind of money I have: you've got to be one lucky son-of-a-gun."

Solomon, in one of his most insightful proverbs, states, **I again saw under the sun that the race is not to the swift, and the battle is not to the warriors, and neither is bread to the wise, nor wealth to the discerning, nor favor to men of ability; for time and chance overtake them all (Ecclesiastes 9:11).** So if we should become disenchanted with our positions in life, if we've just lost that job promotion to someone less qualified, if we have worked diligently at living a good life, have pursued our business endeavors following the best-laid plan, and yet do not seem to be moving forward but are stuck on the treadmill of life, we should not be discouraged and feel singled out as a loser. Even Solomon, in all his wealth and glory, apparently had these same feelings, as have millions of people since. If you arrive at such a point in your career, first review your course and make sure it is the correct one for you personally and not one some- one else has set for you. Secondly, when you have firmly established the correct career course, one based on your own intuition and the advice of counsel and God, then pursue that course fervently, utilizing all the proper business techniques Solomon teaches. But keep these verses in mind:

There is an appointed time for everything, And there is a time for every event under heaven (Ecclesiastes 3:1). For there is a proper time and procedure for every delight, when a man's trouble is heavy upon him. If no one knows what will happen, who can tell him when it will happen. No man has authority to restrain the wind with the wind, or authority over the day of death, and there is no discharge in the time of war, and evil will not deliver those who practice it. {Ecclesiastes 8:6-8}. Moreover, man does not know his time: like fish caught in a treacherous net, and birds trapped in a snare, so the sons of men are ensnared at an evil time when it suddenly falls on them. Also this I came to see as wisdom under the sun, and it impressed me (Ecclesiastes 9:12-13).

As we pursue our course, we must be mindful that life is not always a "walk in the park." We should not be discouraged but forge on, because we can never know when that lucky break may appear. It is our job to be prepared so we can take advantage of the right time when it finally comes. Although it is impossible to control time or circumstance, it is our responsibility to always be ready.

~ Part III ~

Things to Avoid

Introduction

Just as there are characteristics and actions that are positives in developing a business, there are also negatives that Solomon warns against. **There are six things which the Lord hates, Yes, seven which are abomination to Him: Haughty eyes, a lying tongue, And hands that shed innocent blood, A heart that devises wicked plans, Feet that run rapidly to evil, A false witness who utters lies, And one who spreads strife among brothers (Proverbs 6:16-19).**

In addition to these seven traits the Lord hates, Solomon points to seven specific business characteristics and practices that one should avoid if one plans to develop a successful business. The seven are as follows: bribes, arrogance, selfish- ness, gluttony, iniquity, scoffing, and contentiousness.

Bribes

Of the five verses that deal with bribes, two speak of their value and three of their danger. The two verses that address value interchange the connotation of *bribe* with *gift.* **A bribe is a charm in the sight of its owner; wherever he turns, he prospers (Proverbs 17:8). A man's gift makes room for him, And brings him before great men (Proverbs 18:16).** So we begin with the premise that a gift given openly, with nothing expected in return, is a very valuable business tool. But as we proceed through the scriptures, the differences between a gift and a bribe are outlined. **A gift in secret subdues anger, And a bribe in the bosom, strong wrath (Proverbs 21:14).** We are warned that giving a hidden gift (bribe) in order to seek something in return causes trouble. And the more we turn gifts into bribes, the more trouble they become. **The King gives stability to the land by justice, But a man who takes a bribe overthrows it (Proverbs 29:4).** And, finally, Solomon says, **For oppression makes a wise man mad, And a bribe corrupts the heart (Ecclesiastes 7:7).**

While gifts are acceptable in business and work well, there is a fine line between a gift and a bribe. The ability to make this distinction is crucial in avoiding the corruption of one's very heart. If there is ever a question whether something offered is a gift or a bribe, it is better left not given.

Arrogance

The second thing Solomon warns us to avoid is arrogance. **An arrogant man stirs up strife, but he who trusts in the Lord will prosper (Proverbs 28:25)**. Anytime one puts so much confidence in one's own abilities that one doesn't have to depend on the Lord, it becomes arrogance. It is a character trait that is visible and dangerous in business. If one views oneself above needing help, chances are that no one will help, and without help in business it is practically impossible to survive. To avoid strife, avoid arrogance.

Selfishness

Along with arrogance, Solomon warns of selfishness and its dangers. He says, **Do not eat the bread of a selfish man, or desire his delicacies; For as he thinks within himself, so he is. He says to you, 'Eat and drink!' But his heart is not with you. You will vomit up the morsel you have eaten, And waste your compliments (Proverbs 23:6-8).** Solomon warns us to avoid not only arrogance and selfishness but also doing business with others who are arrogant and selfish; all they will cause, to use Solomon's words, are "vomit" and "strife." Business cannot be considered successful and rewarding, no matter how much profit is made, if there is so much strife that it makes one nauseous. It may seem trite, but "the money is not worth the headaches" is a true saying many more times than we are willing to admit.

Gluttony

In modern society, there seems to be so many things that are bad for us and dangerous to us and to our business, that we sometimes overlook a silent sin—gluttony. Most things in life will not hurt you if used in moderation, but the excessive use of anything is terminal. Solomon envisioned the same problems in ancient Jerusalem: **Do not be with heavy drinkers of wine, Or with gluttonous eaters of meat; For the heavy drinker and the glutton will come to poverty, And drowsiness will clothe a man with rags (Proverbs 23:20-21).** So, before you plan to attend that next prime rib-three martini business luncheon, read Proverbs 23: 20-21 and remember as a wise old man once said, "Discussing business over 'wine and prime' is fine, but before I make a decision, I want to think about it over the meat and potatoes."

Iniquity

Solomon says, **He who sows iniquity will reap vanity, And the rod of his fury will perish (Proverbs 22:8)**. Iniquity, or "gross injustice" to quote Webster, is certainly a very dangerous element in business. The real lesson in verse eight is to be fair in all dealings, both personal and professional, so that those with whom one deals will deal justly as well.

Scoffers and Contentious Employees

Solomon warns us to avoid two types of people: scoffers and those who are contentious. The following verses and Solomon's solution would be well-placed if matted, framed, and hung in every company's Human Resources office: **For lack of wood the fire goes out, And where there is no whisperer, contention quiets down. Like charcoal to hot embers and wood to fire, So is a contentious man to kindle strife (Proverbs 26:20-21). Drive out the scoffer, and contention will go out, Even strife and dishonor will cease (Proverbs 22:10).**

Conclusion

This book on business has been written using ancient proverbs that, when combined in a logical sequence, make a tremendous creed to follow in today's business environment. In no way is it a complete usage of Proverbs or Ecclesiastes; for further study, I urge you to read them in their entirety. Solomon him- self says **But beyond this, my son, be warned: the writing of many books is endless, and excessive devotion to books is weary- ing to the body (Ecclesiastes 12:12).**

In conclusion, if I may take from several scriptures and com- bine Solomon's own works from context, I think he offers the perfect synopsis of this work: **There is an evil which I have seen under the sun and it is prevalent among men—a man to whom God has given riches and wealth and honor so that his soul lacks nothing of all that he desires, but God has not empowered him to eat from them, for a foreigner enjoys them. This is vanity and a severe affliction (Ecclesiastes 6:1-2). Even if the other man lives a thousand years twice and does not enjoy good things—do not all go to one place? All a man's labor is for his mouth and yet the appetite is not satisfied (Ecclesiastes 6:6-7). So I commended pleasure, for there is nothing good for a man under the sun except to eat and to drink and to be merry, and this will stand by him in his toils throughout the days of his life which God has given him under the sun (Ecclesiastes 8:15). There is nothing better for a man than to eat and drink and tell himself that his labor is good. This also I have seen, that it is from the hand of God**

(Ecclesiastes 2:24). The conclusion, when all has been heard, is: fear God and keep His commandments, because this applies to every person. For God will bring every act to judgment, everything which is hidden, whether it is good or evil (Ecclesiastes 12:13-14).